Do You Know?

ABOUT

STARS AND PLANETS

By
James Muirden

Illustrated by
Hayward Art Group

Warwick Press
New York/London/Toronto/Sydney
1986

Contents

Astronomy is about space and the things to be found in it, from specks of dust to whole galaxies of stars. It is also about time; some objects are so far away that they are seen now as they were millions of years ago, when the light started on its way.

Space has fascinated people for thousands of years. Astronomers have found out a great deal by using telescopes, but it is only recently that we have been able to send spacecraft to explore the solar system. Was there ever life on the other planets? Will the sun ever burn up the earth? When will the next great comet appear? What are black holes? How did the universe begin? Some of these questions have been answered, but others remain a mystery.

ISBN 0-531-19023-4

Library of Congress Catalog Card No. 86-50787

Published in 1986 by Warwick Press 387 Park Avenue South, New York, New York 10016.
First Published in 1986 by Grisewood and Dempsey Ltd., London
Copyright © by Grisewood and Dempsey Ltd., 1986
Printed in Spain.

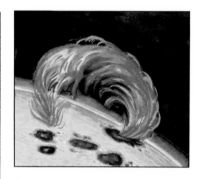

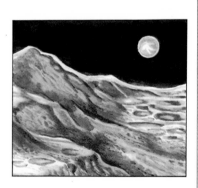

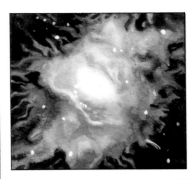
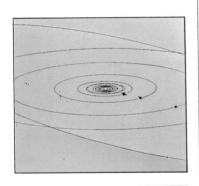

What Is Astronomy About?

Although our planet earth seems so huge and steady to us, it is one of the smallest objects astronomers can make out, and it is flying through space much faster than any spacecraft.

In fact, the earth *is* our spacecraft. It whirls around the sun in its path or orbit once a year, while the sun pulls the earth and its eight neighbor planets with it as it travels along its own path through the universe.

Planet Earth.

The Solar System

The sun and these nine planets make up the *solar system*. However, the sun is just one of millions of other stars in our galaxy. These other stars appear as pinpoints of light, because they are so far away. Yet these stars are huge fiery balls of gas, like our sun.

Our galaxy is shaped like a spiral, with "arms" made of stars and vast clouds of gas and dust. The stars look crowded together, but our nearest neighbor star is about a million times as far away as the sun. The sun's position in the galaxy is shown by the arrow in the picture.

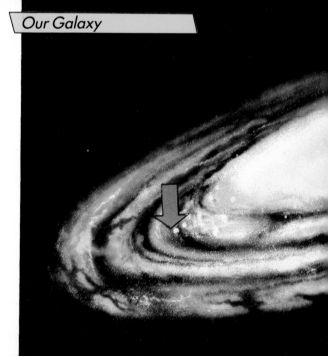

Our Galaxy

4

Distances in astronomy are so huge that astronomers have had to invent special units to measure them. One of these is the *light-year*. A light-year is the distance which a ray of light travels in one year — about six trillion miles!

Light from the sun takes only 8½ minutes to reach us, but the nearest star is over four light-years away. Our galaxy measures about 100,000 light-years across, and the farthest known galaxy is about 15 billion light-years away. The sun and the planets seem very close together in the vastness of space compared to these faraway stars.

Our galaxy is just one of countless millions scattered through the universe. Some are spiral, like ours, but others are round or shapeless. The most distant known ones are only faint specks, even when they are seen through powerful telescopes.

How long does it take for light to reach us from these objects in space?

The moon	1½ seconds
The sun	8½ minutes
The farthest planet in the solar system	5½ hours
The nearest star	4¼ years
The nearest galaxy	2¼ million years
The farthest known galaxy	About 15 billion years

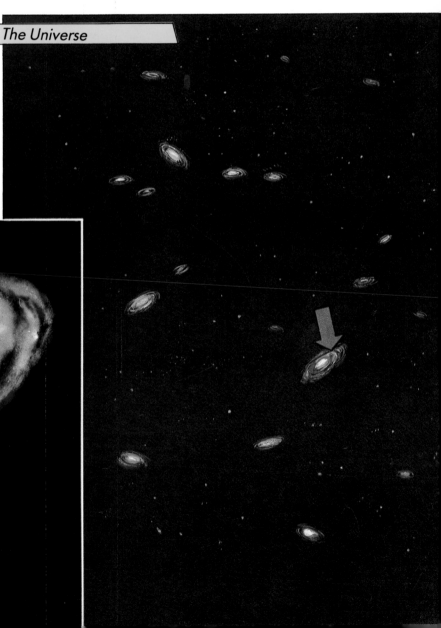

The Universe

② The Expanding Universe

How old is the universe? This is one of the questions that have puzzled astronomers for centuries. It is only recently that they have begun to agree about the answers.

It is obvious that the universe must be at least as old as the solar system, and space explorers have found rocks about four billion years old on the moon. But a more important clue has come from observing distant galaxies, rather than things close by. It turns out that all the galaxies seem to be moving away from each other — in other words, that the universe is expanding.

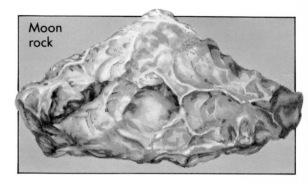

Moon rock

The galaxies do not look as if they are moving — the clue comes from the light they give out. Although the stars appear as tiny specks of light when seen through

The Big Bang

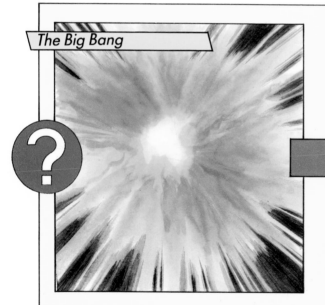

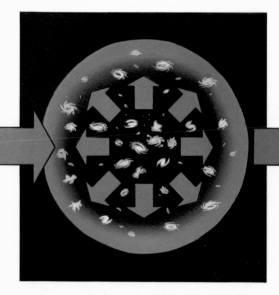

Many astronomers believe that millions of years ago, all the matter in the universe was packed tightly together in a fantastically hot mass. A huge explosion caused all this matter to fly out into space. We call this explosion the "big bang."

As the universe expanded, it cooled down. Vast clouds of gas and dust collected. Stars began to form inside these clouds, which became young galaxies. These galaxies continued to fly away from each other in all directions into space.

even the biggest telescopes, much can be learned about this light when it is passed through a special instrument called a spectroscope. Astronomers observing starlight through a spectroscope discovered that if a star was traveling toward the earth, the light appeared bluish. If a star was traveling away from the earth, the light became slightly red. By measuring how red the galaxies are, their speed can be worked out. The more distant galaxies are moving away faster than the nearer ones, at speeds of more than 62,000 miles every second!

Working back in time, the galaxies must all have been close together about 15 billion years ago. Could this have been the time when the universe began?

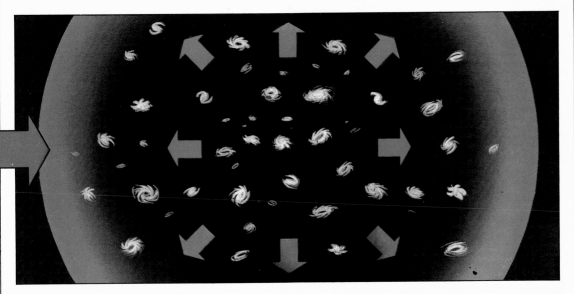

All the galaxies in the universe were probably formed very soon after the big bang. Therefore our own galaxy is about as old as the universe itself, although old stars are dying and new ones are being born inside it all the time.

People have wondered for hundreds of years if the universe has an "edge." But since all the galaxies throughout the universe are flying away from each other on all sides, it is not possible to state where the universe ends, or how big it is.

③ Star Cities – The Galaxies

On a clear night when there is no bright moon, you may see a hazy band of white light stretching across the sky. This is the Milky Way — our view of countless millions of stars inside our galaxy. They seem faint to us only because they are so far away. In fact, many of these stars that look so dim and distant from the earth, are much bigger and brighter than our sun.

When we look at the Milky Way, we are actually looking through the thickest part of our galaxy. The sun lies on the edge of one of the galaxy's spiral arms, and the Milky Way is our view through this and other nearby arms. The brightest part of the Milky Way is in the direction of the center of the galaxy.

From earth, we are only able to see part of our galaxy. If we could see it from far out in space, it would look something like this. At the center is a round swarm of giant stars much brighter than the sun. The spiral arms contain stars mixed with clouds of gas and dust, which are known as *nebulas*. Altogether, there are about 100 billion stars in our galaxy.

Irregular galaxies have no special shape. They contain many bright young stars and plenty of nebulas. These will eventually form new stars, to replace the old ones as they fade and die.

Spiral galaxies turn in space, but take millions of years to go around once. The stars near the center of the galaxy are very old. The arms contain young and old stars, and nebulas.

Elliptical, or oval-shaped galaxies do not contain many nebulas. Some of the largest known galaxies are giant ellipticals, with a hundred times as many stars as the ones in our own galaxy.

The arms of a spiral galaxy contain many bright nebulas like the one shown in the picture. Stars are being born inside them, and these make the gas shine. There are also huge dark dust clouds, which form the "deep-freeze" of material for new stars.

Most of the stars, including ones as bright as the sun, are much too dim to be made out singly from this distance. But a few really brilliant ones do shine out. These may be up to a million times as bright as the sun, and these are known as *white giants* or *blue giants*. *Red giants*, huge puffed-out stars nearing the end of their lives, are also very bright.

The brightest known type of star is not shown here. This is a *supernova*, the explosive death of a giant star, when it blazes out as brightly as an entire galaxy! In 1054, Chinese astronomers saw a star explode like this. Its shattered remains can still be seen in the sky as the beautiful Crab Nebula.

The Life Of A Star

Different Stars

Star Nebula

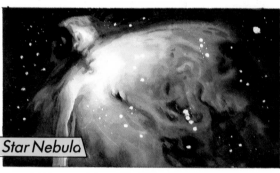

The sun is one among millions of stars in the universe. These stars vary greatly in age. Some are still very young, while others are nearing the end of their life. The sun is a "middle aged" star, being about five billion years old.

Stars are born in clusters inside huge nebulas. The sun probably belonged to a cluster once, but the stars have drifted apart. Many star clusters can be seen in the sky; the Pleiades (or Seven Sisters) are a good example.

Planetary Nebula

White Dwarf

Eventually our sun will begin to expand into a red giant. It will become so hot that life on the earth will die; our planet may even be swallowed up. Toward the end of its life, the star's outer layers drift away into space like a giant smoke ring, called a *planetary nebula.*

The core of the old star remains at the center of the planetary nebula. As the layers float away, the core shrinks down to a very small, hot object — a *white dwarf.* When this happens to our sun, it will shine in our skies like a brilliant point of light — but there will be no one alive in our solar system to see it. A white dwarf has no fuel left, and so it gradually begins to cool down. Billions of years into the future it will fade away and become a black dwarf, and the frozen planets will continue to circle their invisible star.

Some stars contain much more material than the sun. They shine thousands of times more brightly, but use up their hydrogen fuel very quickly. Their lifetime may be "only" a few hundred million years. These are known as *supergiants* (1). A supergiant may finally destroy itself in a stupendous supernova explosion (2), showering its brilliant outer layers into space.

A supernova leaves a shell of shining gas, or planetary nebula (3), perhaps with a tiny *neutron star* at the center. This is so dense that a marble-sized piece would weigh as much as an apartment block!

If the neutron star is dense enough, something extraordinary happens. The strong *gravity* (or "pulling force") at the star's center causes it to pull itself inward. All that remains is a bottomless pit in the universe — a *black hole* (4). A black hole cannot be seen, since it even swallows its own light. It also draws in surrounding gas and dust, as a whirlpool sucks in leaves. Anything that is swallowed by a black hole will be lost forever.

5 The Stars In The Sky

Some stars in the night sky appear to shine more strongly than others. However, some very bright stars seem faint and unremarkable because they are so far away from the earth. The brightest star in the sky, Sirius, is only nine light-years away. Canopus, 1,200 light-years away, sends out far more light — but its tremendous distance from the earth makes it appear fainter than Sirius.

If you look at the stars very carefully, you will see that they are different colors. This tells us how hot they are, since the color of a star depends on the temperature of its surface. The hottest stars are blue-white. Next come yellow stars like the sun, followed by orange and red stars. Some red stars, like Betelgeuse, shine more brightly than a hotter white star like Sirius, because they are so huge.

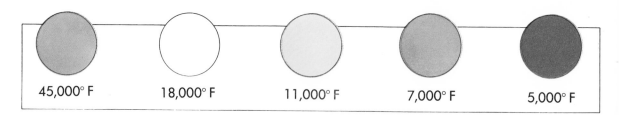

| 45,000° F | 18,000° F | 11,000° F | 7,000° F | 5,000° F |

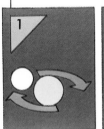
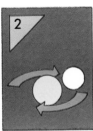
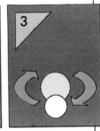

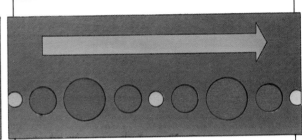

A telescope will show many double or *binary* stars circling around each other. One circuit may take anything from hours to centuries. When seen from earth, one of the stars may vanish behind the other every so often, which dims the brightness of the light we see.

Other *variable* stars change in brightness because they are swelling and shrinking. This cannot be seen, as all stars appear to us as points of light, but special instruments can measure their pulsing. Some swell and shrink regularly, while others flare and dim without warning.

Betelgeuse

Betelgeuse is a red supergiant star 310 light-years away. It is over a hundred times the diameter of the sun, and changes a little in brightness from year to year.

Orion Nebula

The Orion Nebula, 1,300 light-years away, can be seen with the naked eye. It is about 15 light-years across, and new stars are being formed inside it at the moment.

Rigel

Rigel is a white supergiant star 910 light-years away — the light we see left it around the time of the Norman Conquest of Britain in 1066! It is about 40,000 times as bright as the sun, and its surface is about four times as hot.

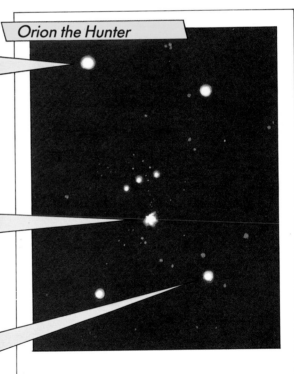

Orion the Hunter

This is the famous star group of Orion the Hunter. It can be seen at some time of the night between October and April.

A Star Called The Sun

All light and warmth on earth comes from the sun. If it failed us, we would be plunged into the freezing blackness of space.

The sun is so huge that a million earths would fit inside it. It is like a vast hydrogen bomb which has not exploded because its gravity holds it together. The temperature at the center is probably about 36 million degrees Fahrenheit, but the surface or *photosphere* is about 11,000 degrees. The patches known as sunspots look black because they are cooler than the surrounding brilliance. Huge arches of glowing hydrogen, called prominences, rise from the photosphere.

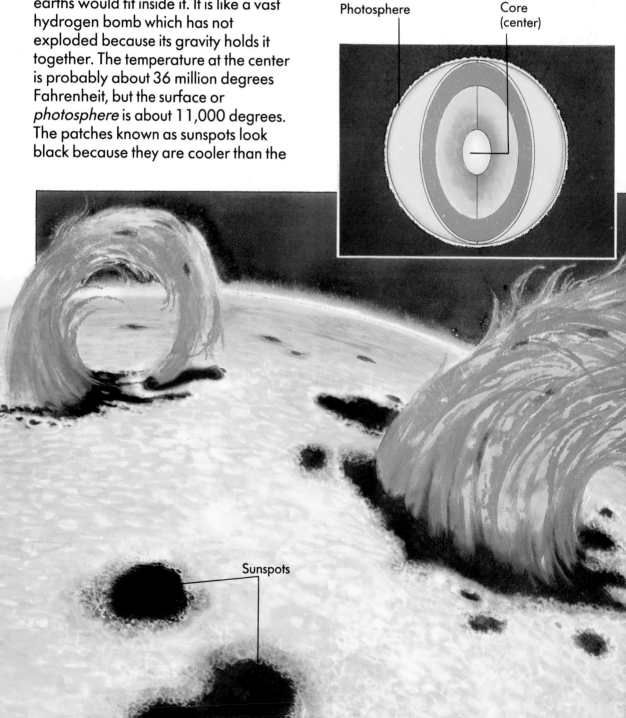

Photosphere

Core (center)

Sunspots

Never look at the sun! Even without a telescope, it can blind you. To observe sunspots, cast a sharp image from a telescope or binoculars onto a white card. Use another card to shade the image from direct sunlight.

If the moon happens to pass exactly in front of the sun, a total eclipse occurs. For a few minutes, the prominences and the faint corona (the hot ring of gases surrounding the sun), shine out in the weird twilight.

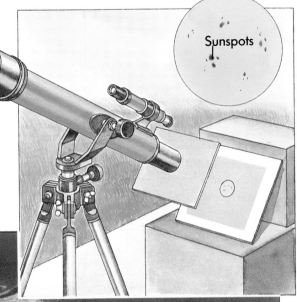

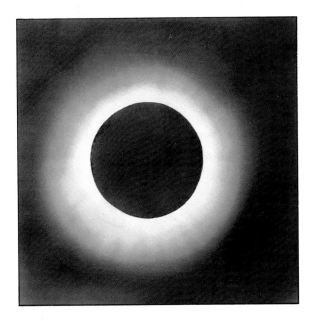

nce

Some sunspots send out invisible sprays of electrified particles, called the solar wind, which can make our atmosphere glow with spectacular bands of light. These displays of auroras are best seen from places near the earth's poles. The particles may also cause interference on our televisions and radios.

7 The Sun's Family

In the night sky, some of the planets shine like stars. But there is a very big difference between them. A planet shines by reflecting the sun's light, while a star is hot and bright. It may seem surprising, then, that the sun and the planets were formed together, in a nebula like this one.

About 4.5 billion years ago, a nebula made up of hydrogen gas and clouds of dust began to shrink into separate stars. One of these stars was the young sun, glowing red. Held by the magnetic force of the sun's gravity, the hazy, half-formed planets circled around in their orbits.

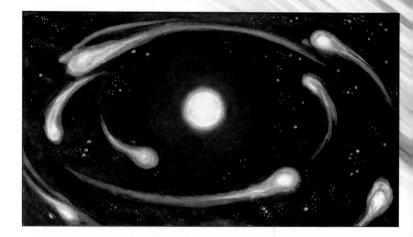

Although the sun quickly came up to its full power, the planets themselves never grew hot enough to shine as stars. But they did become very heated as the pieces of matter in the nebula collided together to form them. Most of the planets had smaller bodies circling them, just as the planets circle around the sun. These are called moons, or satellites.

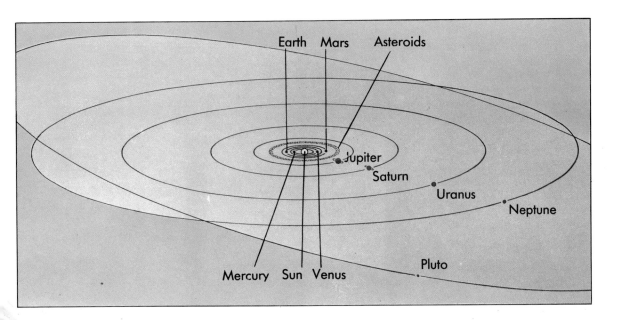

Earth Mars Asteroids

Jupiter

Saturn

Uranus

Neptune

Pluto

Mercury Sun Venus

Asteroid

Comet

The major planets of the solar system seem to form an orderly family, except for tiny Pluto whose enormous orbit is tilted out of line compared to the rest.

The asteroids, or "minor planets," are lumps of rock and metal out in the vast space between Mars and Jupiter. Most are only a few miles across.

There are also the mysterious comets, — icy bodies measuring a few miles across. If they pass near the sun, the ice may turn to gas and stream away in a huge "tail."

Tiny marble-sized bodies swarm around the sun in their millions. They can only be seen if they happen to collide with the earth, and burn up the atmosphere as a meteor or "shooting star."

(8) The Planets

1. Mercury

Distance from sun:
  36 million miles
Time to orbit sun
  (year): 88 days*
Length of day:
  176 days
Diameter: 3,031 miles
Known satellites: 0

2. Venus

Distance from sun:
  67 million miles
Time to orbit sun
  (year): 225 days
Length of day:
  243 days
Diameter: 7,521 miles
Known satellites: 0

3. Earth

Distance from sun:
  93 million miles
Time to orbit sun
  (year): 365 days
Length of day:
  24 hours
Diameter: 7,926 miles
Known satellites: 1

6. Saturn

Distance from sun:
  885 million miles
Time to orbit sun
  (year): 29.5 years
Length of day:
  10 hours 14 minutes
Diameter: 74,567 miles
Known satellites: 24

7. Uranus

Distance from sun:
  1.7 billion miles
Time to orbit sun
  (year): 84 years
Length of day:
  About 16 hours
Diameter: 32,312 miles
Known satellites: 15

8. Neptune

Distance from sun:
  2.8 billion miles
Time to orbit sun
  (year): 165 years
Length of day:
  About 14 hours
Diameter: 30,075 miles
Known satellites: 2

4. Mars

Distance from sun:
   142 million miles
Time to orbit sun
   (year) 687 days
Length of day:
   24 hours 37 minutes
Diameter: 4,222 miles
Known satellites: 2

5. Jupiter

Distance from sun:
   485 million miles
Time to orbit sun
   (year): 11.9 years
Length of day:
   9 hours 50 minutes
Diameter: 88,734 miles
Known satellites: 16

The four inner planets (Mercury, Venus, Earth, and Mars) have a rocky surface. They are not made up of hydrogen, like the giant planets, because they did not have enough gravity to stop the gas from escaping into space at the time when they were forming.

9. Pluto

Distance from sun:
   3.7 billion miles
Time to orbit sun
   (year): 248 years
Length of day:
   6 days 9 hours
Diameter: 1,864 miles
Known satellites: 1

The four giant planets (Jupiter, Saturn, Uranus, and Neptune) are mostly hydrogen, although they are covered with icy clouds of ammonia, methane, and other poisonous gases. Saturn, Jupiter, and Uranus have rings of icy moonlets. Tiny Pluto is a strange, frozen world of its own.

* Figures refer to Earth days

9 The Earth And The Moon

Like the moon, the earth must once have been covered with craters — the huge scars left by flying bodies when they struck these worlds in their youth.

While they were forming, both globes were very hot. But the moon quickly cooled and hardened, preserving the scars. Being much larger, the earth has stayed warm longer. Volcanoes and other movements in the surface crust have all helped to destroy the craters.

Another big difference between the two worlds is the *atmosphere*. There is no air on the moon, because its gravity is not strong enough to hold onto any air. Without air, there can be no life as we know it.

Earth Landscape

The atmosphere is what makes the earth a living planet. Water rises into the air and falls as life-giving rain. The air also absorbs harmful rays from the sun which could kill all known life.

Moon Landscape

The landscape of the moon is a dry desert under a black sky. By day it is boiling hot, and by night it is colder than the earth's poles. A footprint will last unchanged for centuries in this airless world.

The moon appears to shine because it reflects light from the sun. At New Moon (1), its lit-up side is turned away from us and it is invisible. But as it moves around the earth, we see more of its lit-up surface. At First Quarter (2) and Last Quarter (4) it appears as a half. At Full Moon (3), the sunlit side faces us.

As it moves from New to Full, it is said to be waxing (growing bigger). As it moves back to New, it is said to be waning (getting smaller).

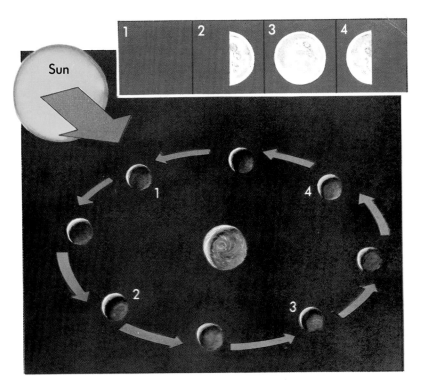

The moon's craters were formed up to four billion years ago by stray rocky bodies crashing to the surface. Some craters are more than 60 miles across. Traveling at 30 miles a second, a body a few hundred feet across could blast a crater as big as a city. In doing so, it would often throw up a mountain in the crater.

⑩ Planets Like The Earth

Little Mercury is the closest planet to the sun. It is cratered like the moon, and the scorching heat roasts one side of its surface to 750 degrees Fahrenheit — hot enough to melt lead and tin. However, on the side of the planet turned away from the sun, the temperature falls well below freezing point. The surface of this tiny airless planet is covered in craters, showing signs of heavy bombardment.

Mercury takes 88 days to circle the sun — the shortest orbit in the solar system. A complete day and night takes 176 earth days, or two of Mercury's years!

Mercury

Venus is a beautiful sight when it shines in the evening or morning twilight, but it is a stifling world shrouded in permanent cloud. The surface temperature is about 930 degrees Fahrenheit, making it the hottest place in the solar system. This is because the clouds let the sun's heat rays pass through, but trap the warmth rising up from the surface.

The atmosphere is so dense that some of the first robot-operated space *probes* to visit it collapsed under its pressure. It consists of poisonous gases and droplets of acid. No known forms of life could survive the grim conditions of this hostile planet.

Venus

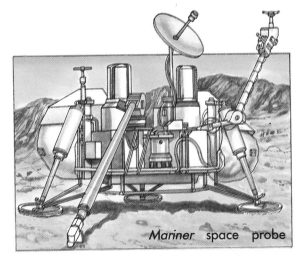

Mariner space probe

The faint hope that there was life on Mars ended when two *Mariner* space probes sampled the surface conditions in 1976. Mars turned out to be a freezing desert with hardly any atmosphere. Strong winds blow rusty-colored dust into the sky, turning it pink.

As well as carrying the scars of craters, Mars has been shaken by earthquakes and volcanoes. One volcano, now no longer active, is Mount Olympus. This is three times as high as Mount Everest, while a huge gash in the surface known as Mariner Valley could stretch right across the United States!

Mars

(11) The Frozen Giants

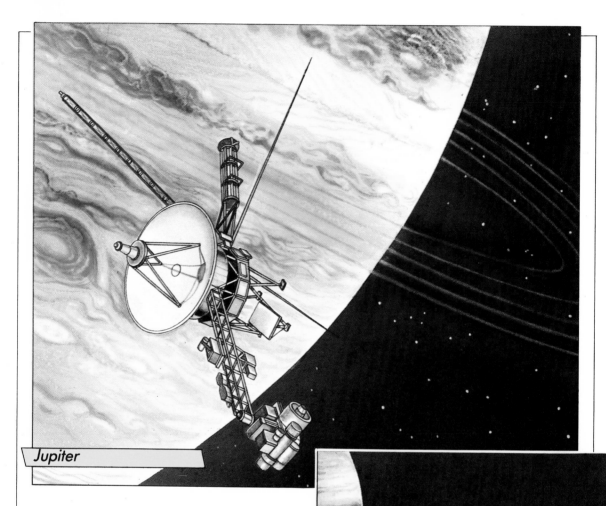

Jupiter

Jupiter, the first and largest of the giant planets, orbits the sun in the chill outer regions of the solar system. It is so large that all the other planets and their moons could fit inside it.

Jupiter's "surface" is just the upper layer of swirling gas clouds. These rise and fall and mingle with each other, while different chemicals tint them in fantastic colors. The famous Great Red Spot seems to be a permanent whirlwind among these ever-changing cloud forms.

Jupiter has four important satellites and at least 12 tiny ones. One of the large ones, Io, is covered by active volcanoes. The icy surface of Europa makes it shine brightly, while Callisto is pitted by craters. Ganymede is the largest satellite in the solar system. Jupiter also has faint rings of sulfur and ice.

Saturn is the most spectacular planet in the solar system. As well as its many moons, it has several thousand gleaming rings that measure 23 times the earth's diameter from side to side.

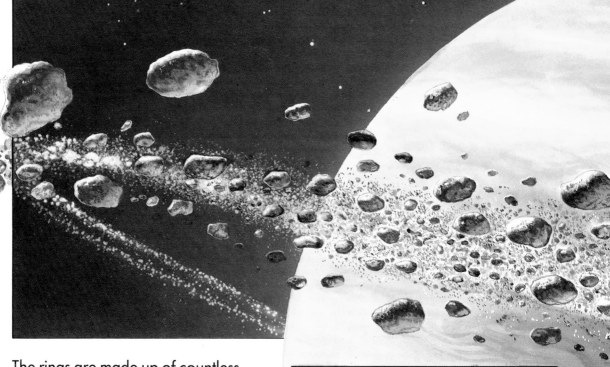

The rings are made up of countless millions of icy moonlets, a couple of feet across. Some parts of the ring are more crowded than others, and are therefore brighter. The rings are so thin that they disappear from view when they appear edge-on as seen from earth.

Titan, the largest of the 24 known moons, is almost as large as Jupiter's Ganymede. Any spacecraft landing there would see a red sky caused by its nitrogen atmosphere, and a surface made up of rock and ice.

Titan

12 The Outer Planets

Uranus

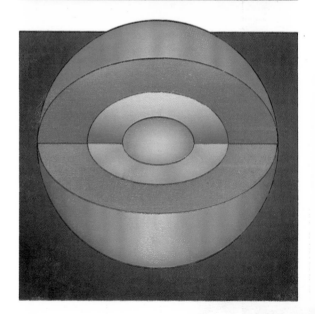

Uranus is less than half the diameter of Jupiter and Saturn, but it is still four times the diameter of the earth! It is so far from the sun that it can hardly be seen with the naked eye at all. It was the first planet to be discovered with a telescope, in 1781.

The space probe *Voyager 2* flew past it in January 1986, and discovered that it has a dense and poisonous atmosphere, 328 degrees below zero. Uranus has a small solid core, covered in icy layers of hydrogen, helium, and methane gas. There are also dozens of very narrow faint rings, not at all like Saturn's bright broad ones. Uranus revolves around the sun tipped over on its side, with the ring system almost upright in space; each pole gets sunlight and darkness for about forty years at a stretch!

Neptune

Pluto is so faint that astronomers had to spend years hunting for it. They thought that the pull of gravity of a large unknown planet was making Neptune wander from its right path — but Pluto is smaller than our moon! Does this mean that there is a tenth planet yet to be discovered?

Pluto has a satellite called Charon, half its own diameter. These little worlds whirl along a strange path — for 20 of the 248 years it takes them to orbit the sun, they are closer to us than Neptune. This will be the case until 1999. Even the largest telescopes on earth show Pluto as a tiny speck, but seen from Charon, it would appear large and pale against the distant stars.

Neptune, slightly smaller than Uranus, is probably a close twin — a huge, ice-clouded world, and at present the farthest planet from the sun. Even a very big telescope cannot make Neptune appear larger than a tiny spot.

Pluto

(13) Comets And Meteors

Comets are made up of loose pieces of dust and rock, held together by frozen gas. They orbit the sun just like the planets, but their path takes them far out to the frozen limits of the solar system for much of their lives. However, as they pass near the sun, the center or *nucleus* begins to glow. The part we see is the cloudy *coma*, which is given off when the sun warms the nucleus. A spectacular tail of gas and dust, millions of miles long, may also develop. Some comets shine in the skies for many weeks. Their tails are thin, and stars may be seen through them.

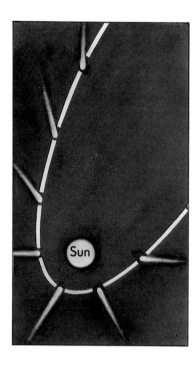

A flow of electrified particles from the sun makes a comet's tail point away from the sun.

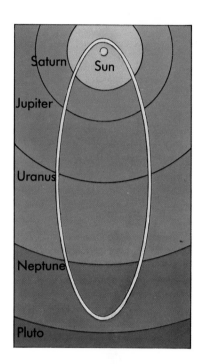

Halley's Comet orbits the sun every 76 years. It can be closer than Venus, and farther than Neptune.

Nucleus

Coma

Tail of gas and dust

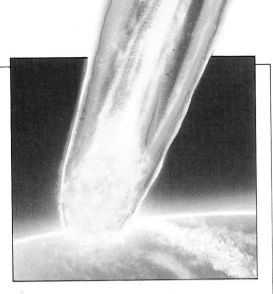

A meteor is the streak of light seen when a particle the size of a marble hurtles into our atmosphere at a speed of more than 30 miles a second. These particles are known as meteoroids. They orbit the sun like minute planets. Some are waste fragments thrown out in swarms by comets. If the earth passes through a swarm of this kind, a meteor shower is seen.

A very large body will pass through the atmosphere and hit the ground. This is known as a meteorite. In 1908, a big meteorite fall in Siberia blew down thousands of trees.

Meteor Crater, in Arizona, was probably blasted out about 25,000 years ago. Half a mile across and more than 650 feet deep, it is the best-preserved meteorite crater on the earth's surface.

(14) Exploring The Sky

You can become an astronomer without owning a telescope. It is often possible to see the nearest planets with the naked eye, and every night a few meteors flash across the sky. With the help of a pair of binoculars, you will be able to see many more stars — including distant galaxies, and nebulas where stars are being born. Binoculars will also show the moon's largest craters.

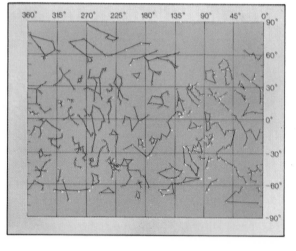

Use binoculars with a magnification of 8 or 10 times. Focus them carefully, so the stars appear as points of light. If they are always blurred, or have bright colors around them, the binoculars are faulty. Support your elbows on something solid, like a wall or the back of a chair, or the stars will dance about.

It is hard to compare a star chart with the sky if you don't know how much sky it shows. The chart should indicate how many degrees of sky it measures along each side. Compare this with the sky by holding up your outspread hand at arm's length; the width of your hand is about 20 degrees.

Watch the moon with binoculars, using this map to identify its craters and the lowland areas known as "seas." They are always in the same position because the moon keeps the same face toward the earth, but their appearance changes as the sun rises and sets over them. Full Moon is not a good time to observe — it is so dazzling that most craters are hard to see.

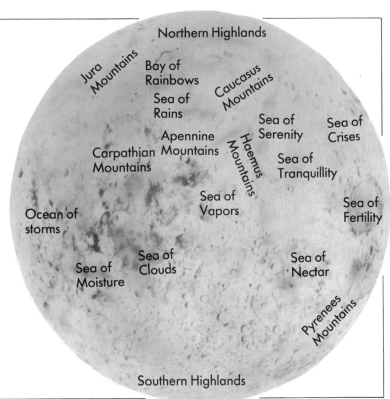

Northern Highlands

Jura Mountains
Bay of Rainbows
Caucasus Mountains
Sea of Rains
Sea of Serenity
Sea of Crises
Apennine Mountains
Carpathian Mountains
Haemus Mountains
Sea of Tranquillity
Sea of Vapors
Sea of Fertility
Ocean of storms
Sea of Moisture
Sea of Clouds
Sea of Nectar
Pyrenees Mountains

Southern Highlands

Radio waves are sent out by everything from planets to galaxies. Some of the most distant galaxies were discovered by radio telescopes, which use a special dish to reflect the waves onto a receiver. Some dishes are more than 900 feet across.

Computer-controlled spacecraft have given us close-up views of most of the planets in the solar system. They can also observe objects farther out in space from above the earth's atmosphere, which dims our view of the universe.

31

Index